HIROSHIMA TO NAGASAKI: PEACE JOURNEY

SOOJA GEN

First published in the UK in October 2025 by
Journey Books, an imprint of Bradt Travel Guides Ltd
31a High Street, Chesham, Buckinghamshire, HP5 1BW, England
www.bradtguides.com

Text copyright © 2025 Sooja Gen
Photos copyright © 2025 individual photographers (see below)

Edited by BBR Design, UK
Cover design by Ian Spick, Bradt Travel Guides
Layout and typesetting by BBR Design, UK
Maps by David McCutcheon FBCart.S
Crane illustration by Shutterstock/Natata
Timeline illustrations by Hanako Kuriyama
Production managed by Sue Cooper, Bradt & Page Bros

The right of Sooja Gen to be identified as the author of this work has been asserted by her in accordance with the Copyright, Designs & Patents Act 1988.

All rights reserved. All views expressed in this book are the views of the author and not those of the publisher. No part of this book may be reproduced, scanned or distributed by any means without the written permission of Bradt Travel Guides, nor used or reproduced in any way to train artificial intelligence technologies/models. Bradt Travel Guides and the author unequivocally reserve this work from the text and data mining exception, as per Article 4(3) of the Digital Single Market Directive 2019/790.

ISBN: 9781804693834

British Library Cataloguing in Publication Data
A catalogue record for this book is available from the British Library

Photographers credited beside images and also those from
libraries credited as follows: Alamy.com (A); Shutterstock.com (S);
SuperStock.com (SS); Wikimedia Commons (WC)

Front cover: The Peace Statue in the Peace Park in Nagasaki (SOOJA GEN)
Back cover: The Children's Peace Monument in Hiroshima (MIRKO KUZMANOVIC/S)

Digital conversion by www.dataworks.co.in
Printed in the UK by Page Bros

To find out more about our Journey Books imprint,
visit www.bradtguides.com/journeybooks

Dedication

I would like to dedicate this book to all people suffering in the many global conflict zones. When so much of their community is destroyed, they must feel that the world has forgotten them. Wars are cruel and devastating, severely shortening lives. Japan experienced all that and yet she recovered, even from the nuclear destruction and desolation. Within a few decades after the unconditional surrender in 1945, the Japanese people recovered enough to host a summer Olympics in 1964.

I pay a special tribute to the Japanese photographer, Yotsugi Kawahara, who captured the destruction of Hiroshima. His photograph of the Hiroden streetcar wreckage became one of the enduring images of the city following the atom bomb.

Today, Japan is a full democracy and governed by the rule of law. Although there may be imperfections in politics, Japan's example may give hope to nations in conflict.

My deepest gratitude goes to David, my husband. Without his support this book would not have been possible. I am also forever grateful to my daughter Hannah.

Contents

Foreword — vii
About Japan — ix
Japanese history timeline — xiii
A journey of discovery from Hiroshima to Nagasaki — xvi

Hiroshima: Japan in microcosm — 1
Miyajima: Entry to Japan's spiritual and samurai heritage — 11
Kure: From naval powerhouse to peaceful port town — 14
The Seto Inland Sea: A gateway to Japan's rich tapestry — 19
Onomichi: A timeless port town and a portal to adventure — 24
Shimanami Kaido: Japan's scenic island-hopping trail — 28
Imabari: The Sea Castle and industry — 31
Ohenro pilgrimage: A route for devotion and reflection — 34
Uchiko: A step back in time — 39
Usuki: A history of maritime encounters — 42

Beppu: Japan's hot spring paradise	51
Kokura: A city of resilience and reflection	54
Fukuoka City: Kyushu's vibrant capital	59
Genkainada: Vital and historical sea of northern Kyushu	68
Hirado: Japan's portal to the West	73
Sasebo: From fishing village to naval powerhouse	79
Dejima: Enter Japan's closed past	82
Nagasaki: A city of faith, trade and resilience	88
From Hiroshima to Nagasaki: A tale of bonds across an ocean	100
Reflection: A rainy pilgrimage to Nagasaki Peace Park	102
The Peace Statue	105
Epilogue: Kindness in the floating world	108

Foreword

This book reveals Japan through its rich history, vibrant culture, key characters and fascinating landscapes. Imagine each story as a bead on a necklace, joining together insights that will help you appreciate Japan as a gem of the East – understanding the Land of the Rising Sun from a new perspective.

Historical and political analysis is for scholars. However, in the current period of global conflict, with peace and stability under threat, the strength and unity of people worldwide have never been more essential. Japan is one such resilient nation, a country that has withstood the trials of war and nuclear devastation. Throughout, it has managed to retain its identity and sovereignty. Japan has never been colonised, a fact which testifies to the immortal spirit of its people.

What is the secret of the nation's strength and ingenuity? This pilgrimage traces a route from Hiroshima to Nagasaki, stopping over in cities and towns in Honshu, Shikoku and Kyushu. You will discover some of the building blocks and underlying spirit of the enduring and sophisticated people of Japan. More than a mere tour, this is a Peace Journey, and I invite you, the reader, to become inspired by the experience of one nation and its people to appreciate the enduring beauty of our shared home on Earth.

About Japan

Japan is an archipelago shaped by the meeting of four tectonic plates. The combined land mass exceeds that of Germany or the British Isles, and is surrounded by the Pacific Ocean, the Sea of Japan, the Sea of Okhotsk and the East China Sea. Japanese land and the sea territories both provide a rich variety of nature and geology, notably 110 live volcanoes, including Mount Fuji.

The ground under Japan is active with magmatic and seismic movements, resulting in several hundred shakes a year, large and small. Visitors typically experience one or two minor tremors during their stay. Sometimes earthquakes cause serious damage, with a risk of tsunamis near the coast. Despite the danger, the fact that Japan is populous, supporting a population of over 120 million, demonstrates that the people have adapted well throughout its long history. On the plus side are the huge number of hot springs, creating perhaps the most famous bathing culture in the world.

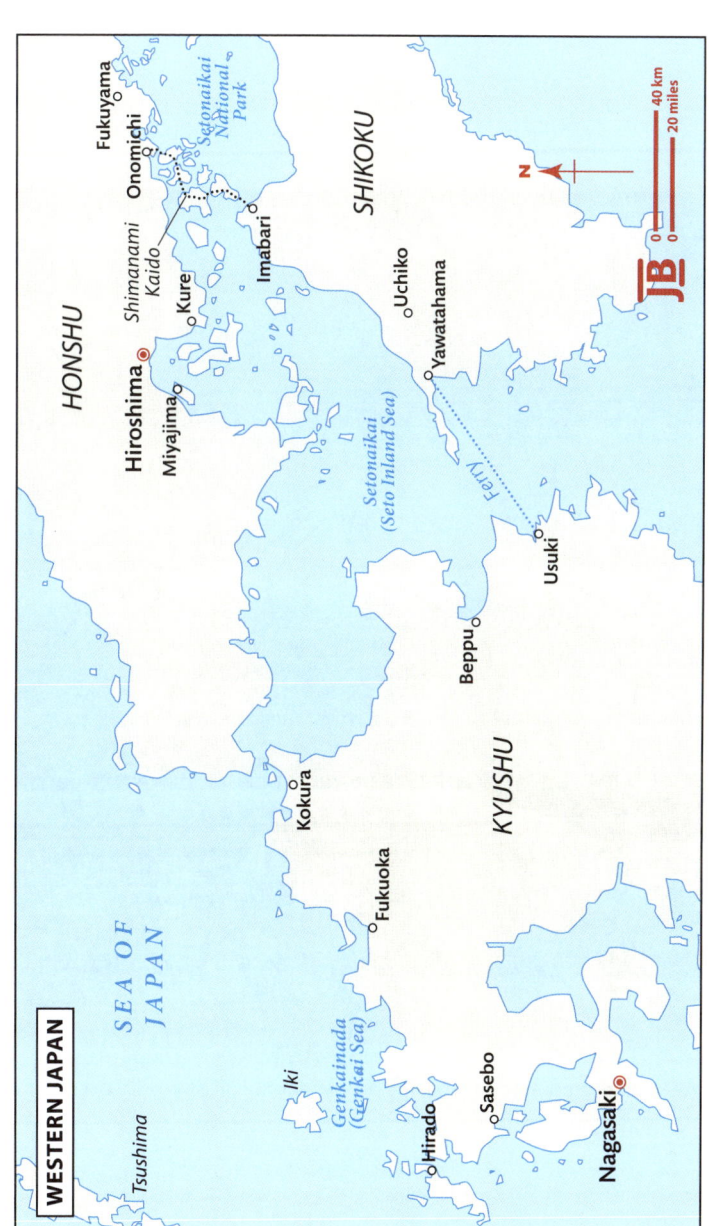

A Shinkansen bullet train passes below Mount Fuji (SEAN PAVONE/S)

Japanese history timeline

*c.*10,000 BCE　縄文 Jomon

*c.*500 BCE　弥生 Yayoi

300 CE　古墳 Kofun

593　飛鳥 Asuka

710　奈良 Nara

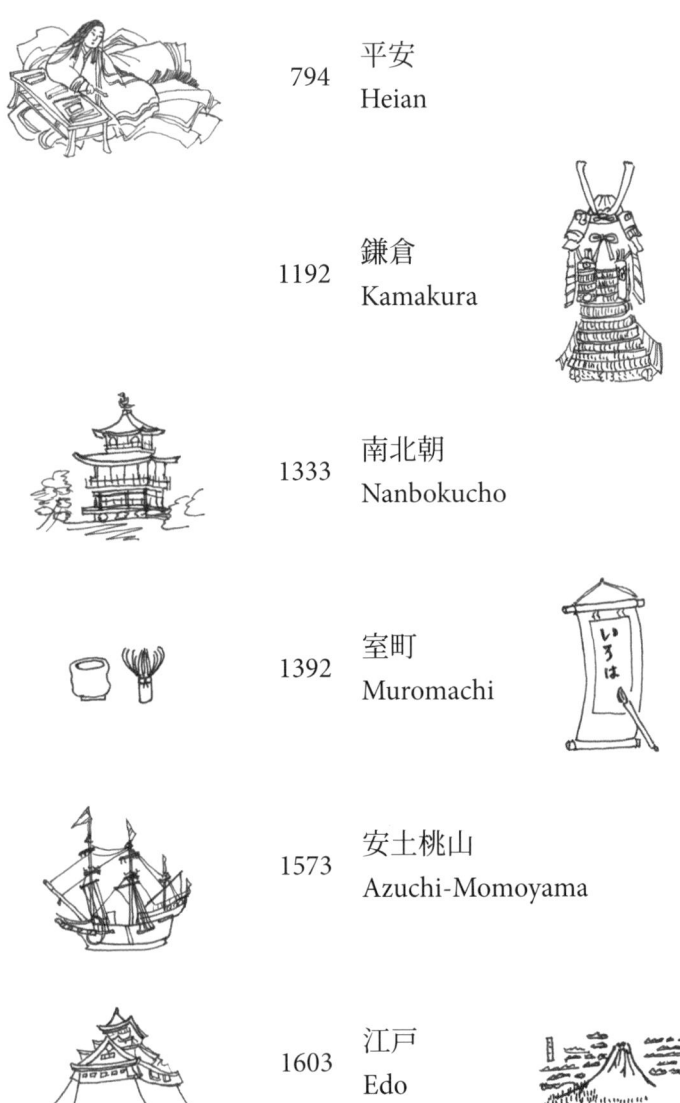

794 平安
Heian

1192 鎌倉
Kamakura

1333 南北朝
Nanbokucho

1392 室町
Muromachi

1573 安土桃山
Azuchi-Momoyama

1603 江戸
Edo

JAPANESE HISTORY TIMELINE

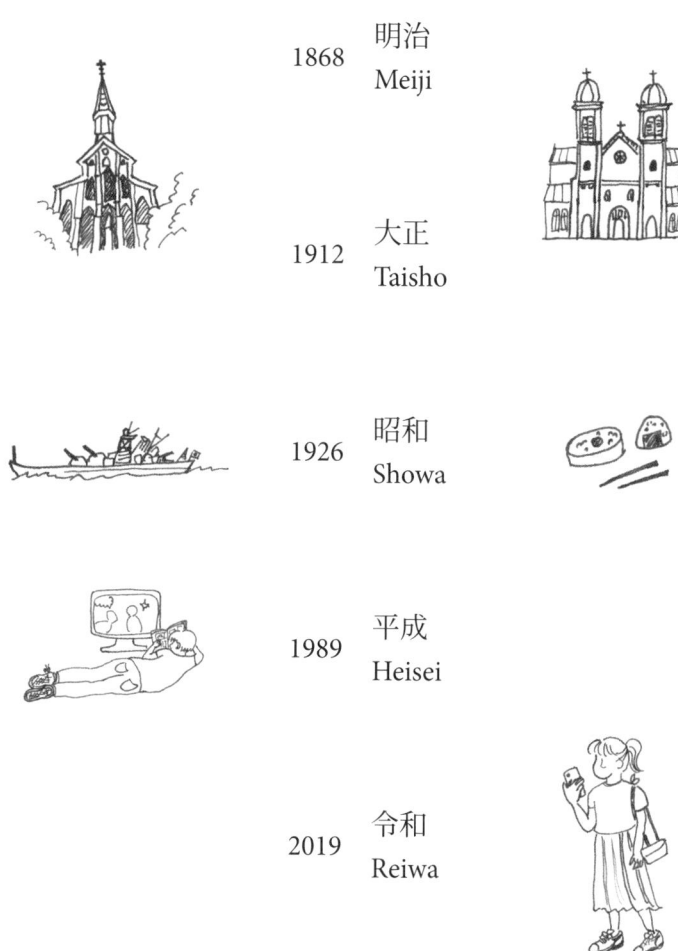

1868　明治
　　　 Meiji

1912　大正
　　　 Taisho

1926　昭和
　　　 Showa

1989　平成
　　　 Heisei

2019　令和
　　　 Reiwa

A journey of discovery from Hiroshima to Nagasaki

This pilgrimage across the western side of Japan begins in Hiroshima and takes you to Nagasaki, travelling through the historic samurai city of Kokura in Kyushu. For those who are familiar with twentieth-century Japanese history, the name Kokura may ring a bell. It was the initial target of the atom bomb known as Fat Man, rather than Nagasaki; the adverse weather conditions on that fateful day decided the second victim of the two atom bombs, so saving Kokura. It is ironic that Nagasaki paid the price for that nuclear attack, because the city was home to the majority of Japan's Christians, who were sympathetic to Western civilisation.

You may also be surprised to learn that migrants from Hiroshima, the first-ever target of a nuclear bomb, had a special role in establishing ties between Japan and the USA. Encouraged by the new Meiji government, by the 1920s migrants from Hiroshima formed the largest immigrant group in Hawaii; many of these second-generation Japanese acquired American citizenship. But how did the people of Hiroshima and Nagasaki, as well as the rest of the Japanese population, regard the country that destroyed so many of their cities and livelihoods? As our pilgrimage unfolds, our journey is as much about healing as it is about discovery, tracing the path to peace across these remarkable cities.

Hiroshima: Japan in microcosm

The capital city of its prefecture, Hiroshima is in many ways a miniature version of Japan: mountainous, yet having a long stretch of coastline. (In fact, Japan has a longer coastline than the USA.) The fertile land produces a great variety of vegetables and fruits, while the Seto Inland Sea, which faces Hiroshima, also provides a rich source of seafood, including oysters.

Hiroshima is diverse, industrious and has its own strong cultural heritage. The local dialect, Hiroshima-ben, is different from that spoken in Fukuoka, Kyoto or Osaka. Many conversational phrasings end in '-jyakee' or its stressed form '-ken' (it sounds the same as 'sword'), and '-no' or '-nya' endings make the dialect quite rhythmical. Referring to 'I am', they use 'washi'; the bird of prey 'eagle' is pronounced the same. The Hiroshima intonation is very different from standard Tokyo Japanese, and some say that the way Hiroshima people speak is a bit macho-sounding but quite relaxed.

The culinary speciality here is **Okonomiyaki** ('cook in the way you like it'), a savoury pancake brimming with ingredients such as noodles, vegetables and seafood or meat. It is an inexpensive street food and very filling. Locals take pride in supporting the numerous okonomiyaki restaurants, whose number per capita surpasses those found in Tokyo or Osaka. The company behind the beloved Otafuku sauce, popular throughout Japan, has its head office in Hiroshima.

Hiroshima Prefecture is the eleventh largest in Japan. With a population of 2.8 million it compares in size to countries like Armenia, Jamaica, Lithuania or Qatar. Hiroshima City, with 1.2 million people alone (about 40% of the prefectural total), is the capital of a region that includes the prefectures of Okayama, Tottori, Shimane and Yamaguchi. Currently, the UK's second-largest city, Birmingham, has a similar population to that of Hiroshima City.

The city's history is of course overshadowed by the devastation of the atom bomb, nicknamed **Little Boy**, in 1945. According to the published statistics, the population dramatically reduced to 135,197 in 1945 from the 343,968 registered in 1940. It is well acknowledged that we do not really know the accurate number of casualties caused by the effect of the bomb. Some vaporised instantly, while others endured a lingering death in the following months and years due to the high level of radiation exposure. However, the people of Hiroshima have shown such resilience despite the apocalyptic destruction of their city.

Hiroden, the Hiroshima Dentetsu tram network established in 1910, has been providing the public with

A Hiroden streetcar, six days after it was burned out by the atom bomb that exploded 300m away on 6 August 1945
(YOTSUGI KAWAHARA/HIROSHIMA PEACE MEMORIAL MUSEUM)

vital transportation in the city almost every day for more than a hundred years. On 6 August 1945, 451 employees, almost 40% of Hiroden's workforce at the time, were killed or injured by the atom bomb. Of its 123 streetcars, 108 were incapacitated. Remarkably, within three days, salvaging what remained, Hiroden restarted although with a very limited service. Today, Hiroden boasts Japan's longest and busiest tram network, with the recent direct connection to the JR Hiroshima bullet train station promising even greater accessibility.

The **Mazda Motor Corporation**, another Hiroshima hallmark, traces its roots back to a cork-making business founded by the Fuchu-based industrialist Mr Matsuda in 1920. Over the decades, the company evolved into a major motor manufacturer and a leader in automotive innovation. Today, it is still headquartered in Fuchu. The Matsuda family, together with the Mazda automotive company, are substantial shareholders and major sponsors of the Hiroshima Toyo Carp, the professional baseball team that competes in the Central League of Nippon Professional Baseball. The Carp are named after the koi fish that climb the rapids around Hiroshima Castle. The Hiroshima Carp team was formed in 1949, only four years after the end of World War II, and is often considered a symbol of the post-war spirit of Hiroshima's revival and eternal optimism.

Koi carp (SOOJA GEN)

Opened in 2009, the impressive Mazda Stadium has a capacity of 32,000 and is only a ten-minute walk from Hiroshima station. Comparable to the England Football team (the Lions, not the Lionesses), the Carps' performances in the Central League create frequent anxiety for their supporters. Nonetheless, the Hiroshima people support their home team with passion.

Equally passionate are the local artists: calligraphers, designers, koto makers and other artisans are drawn to Hiroshima in their droves. The koto is a Japanese stringed instrument, made of Paulownia wood and about 2m long. If you ever hear 'Sakura Sakura' ('cherry blossom, cherry blossom'), one of the most quintessential Japanese melodies, the accompanying musical instrument is often a koto. Fukuyama, an active port on the Seto Inland Sea with the second-largest population after Hiroshima City, and with a rich history as a castle town from the Edo period, has been producing the finest kotos for centuries. Mr Fujii is one such grand master whose kotos fetch millions of yen because of his outstanding craftsmanship. Each year on 10 May, locals celebrate the Koto-no-Hi, honouring this ancient musical instrument. In July, a koto performance

LEFT Hiroshima Castle (SOOJA GEN)

The koto, a traditional Japanese musical instrument (KITREEL/S)

competition is held in Fukuyama, with competitors drawn from all over Japan.

Hiroshima Prefecture was once the number one producer of brushes, particularly in the town of **Kumano** where **fude** (brush) making has been perfected over many generations. **Shodo** (writing with a fude) used to be a compulsory skill taught at school in Japan, and a fude was the main writing instrument before pens and pencils were introduced from the West. Shodo for the Japanese is the Western equivalent of calligraphy. As such it is not just

RIGHT Collections of fude brushes for calligraphy (top), painting (middle) and cosmetics (bottom) (KUMANO, HIROSHIMA PREFECTURE)

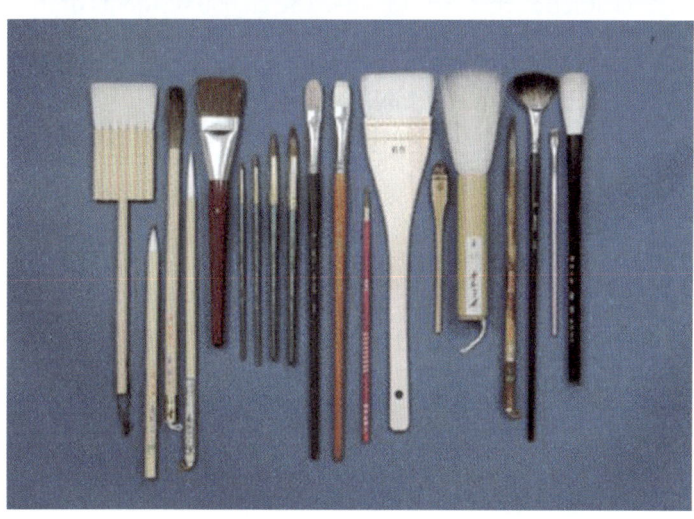

writing, but an art form that reflects the writer's aesthetics and personality. Therefore, a fude which gives good control and flow is important and people are prepared to pay a high price.

The fude from Kumano, made from animal hairs such as horse, rabbit or weasel, or from bird feathers, is renowned for its quality, being favoured by calligraphers, painters and even cosmetic artists worldwide. The 23,000 residents of the town of Kumano include highly skilled artisans dedicated to keeping this tradition alive, and they welcome aspiring learners eager to master the craft. Around the autumn equinox every year, the Fude-matsuri festival takes place in Kumano, including Shodo demonstrations and festival stalls (some of them offer bargain sale prices). If you are prepared to dedicate some years to learning, there is a certificate course which is recognised by the Japanese government. For those who dare to take such a challenge, apply and see if you can become a craftsperson yourself.

Miyajima: Entry to Japan's spiritual and samurai heritage

Just a short ferry ride away, nestled within Hiroshima Bay, you'll find one of Japan's most iconic and sacred islands, **Itsukushima**, also known as **Miyajima**. On approaching it, you are welcomed by the magnificent red **Torii Gate**, rising 15m above the water and marking your entry into a realm of ancient Shinto worship. To this day, burials are forbidden here, so the island has no graveyard. Wild deer roam, often greeting visitors. They love to eat paper, so keep a close guard on your maps, tickets and notes!

Miyajima is home to the **Itsukushima Jinja** shrine, a UNESCO World Heritage Site. It houses cherished artefacts designated by the Japanese government as national treasures, including handwritten manuscripts of revered Buddhist sutras. In Japan, it's common for a shrine and a temple to be built close together, sometimes within the same precinct:

people see nothing unusual about shrines and temples coexisting, their precepts of ideas and beliefs intertwining.

Itsukushima Jinja's most significant contributor was Taira-no-Kiyomori, a twelfth-century warlord who consolidated and expanded the Taira clan and gained total control of Itsukushima in 1168. Kiyomori honoured the Shinto gods of navigation because the Taira family was heavily involved with maritime trade along the Inland Sea, making them rich and powerful.

The Taira clashed with and were defeated by the Minamoto clan during the **Genpei Gassen** civil war (1180–85). The victor, Minamoto-no-Yoritomo, declared himself **shogun**, the highest office of the warrior class. He became the de facto ruler of Japan, and moved the seat of power from Kyoto to Kamakura, the city famous for its 11m-high **Great Buddha**. Here begins the age of the *bushi* samurai, which lasted for seven hundred years until the final shogun, Tokugawa Yoshinobu (1837–1913), lost power in 1868. During the Tokugawa shogunate, Edo, now known as Tokyo, became the capital of Japan.

LEFT The Torii Gate of Miyajima (FRANNNNNK WU/S)

Kure:
From naval powerhouse
to peaceful port town

Kure, in Hiroshima Prefecture, stood as one of Japan's mightiest naval fortresses from where the Imperial Navy launched many operations. At its peak, the population of this bustling port soared past 400,000, attracting elite designers, draftsmen, engineers and auxiliary workers, tirelessly engaged in producing ships, aeroplanes and munitions.

Kure was both confident and magnificent. Here was constructed the pride of Japan's World War II fleet, the massive battleship *Yamato*, 263m in length and weighing 72,000 tons, which briefly served as the flagship of Japan's Combined Fleet in 1942. However, the fortunes of the *Yamato* and of Kure itself changed dramatically following Japan's pre-emptive strike on Pearl Harbor in Honolulu, Hawaii in December 1941, and the *Yamato* was lost en route to Okinawa in April 1945 after relentless strikes by American forces.

The *Yamato*'s equally massive sister battleship **Musashi**, built by Mitsubishi Heavy Industries in Nagasaki, didn't fare well either: sunk in October 1944 by an estimated 19 torpedoes, it is now an archaeological site beneath the Sibuyan Sea in the Philippines.

During the **Pacific War** (1941–45), Kure suffered repeated air raids which destroyed all capabilities as a military base. The neighbouring Hiroshima City was spared from such aerial bombardments: while Kure was burning, Hiroshima was earmarked for the first military use of an atom bomb known as **Little Boy**, so that the effect of this new weapon on a population could be observed.

The *Yamato* (left) and *Musashi* (right) in early 1943 (NIDAY PICTURE LIBRARY/A)

The ferry port in Kure City (M AL FATIH/S)

After the war, Kure played a new role as the operational base for the headquarters of the British Commonwealth Occupation Force. In fact, Japan's relationship with the UK has a much more intricate history than is commonly acknowledged. Sometimes as a friendly country, sometimes as an enemy country, the two nations have been exchanging official documents for over four hundred years. It is interesting to find that Japan chose to emulate the British Navy and that the core design of the *Yamato* was modelled on a British battleship.

The tremendous upheavals endured by the townsfolk during the war is depicted in *In This Corner of the World*, a 2016 award-winning animation by Katabuchi Sunao, which was based on a work of the same title by the female manga artist Kono Fumiyo. However, the Kure it depicts is long gone: the glittering naval base is only a memory, lost beneath the waves. With a reduced population of 200,000, Kure has transformed into a serene community which has retained its shipbuilding industry: the engineering skills survive.

Modern-day Kure's reputation revolves around its culinary offering and thriving sake breweries, such as **Sempuku** (*A Thousand Good Fortunes*). Celebrating the centenary of its naval heritage, the Kure Foods Association has recently produced a guidebook featuring over a hundred eateries in downtown Kure. It is a blessing indeed that Kure is promoting its culinary delights and accompanying sake drinks. These days the local authorities and communities are putting more emphasis on their cultural heritage and civic activities than the area's militaristic past.

Today, Kure port provides popular ferry connections between Hiroshima City and Matsuyama on Shikoku Island, and the ferry terminal that occupies the seafront is surrounded by fascinating vistas. The Yamato Museum stands in the adjoining block, where visitors can explore the town's naval legacy and enjoy the calming views of the Seto Inland Sea, framed by seasonal blooms and Kure's symbols: the camellia flower and oak tree.

The Seto Inland Sea: A gateway to Japan's rich tapestry

The Seto Inland Sea, **Setonaikai** in Japanese, is a fertile stretch of water bordered by three of Japan's main islands: Honshu, Shikoku and Kyushu. Together with Hokkaido in the north, these are the four main islands of the Japanese archipelago. The strong and fast-moving tides support a thriving aquatic ecosystem, said to nurture over a thousand species of fish and shellfish. This sea has historically served as Japan's natural 'fish farm', while also providing a vital maritime highway connecting many ports in the area. Goods have long been traded across these waters, reaching and enriching the historic cities of Kyoto and Nara. The tides, forever shifting, mirror the ebb and flow of Japan's own rich history.

In the twentieth century, Setonaikai inspired a wave of talented female writers, poets and musicians who,

against a background of male chauvinism, gave voice to the emotions and spirit of the time. **Hayashi Fumiko** (1903–51) was prominent among them, capturing coastal lives in her writings such as *Horoki, a Diary of a Vagabond* and *The Accordion and the Fish Town*.

    Tsuboi Sakae (1899–1967) wrote *Twenty-Four Eyes* (1952), which was dramatised in a film of the same name in 1954. Set against the backdrop of Shodoshima, a small island in the Setonaikai, the novel describes how ordinary people – especially children – struggled during World War II. While the imperialistic government persisted with its desperate campaigns in the Pacific and elsewhere, the weakest layer of society was forced to endure deprivation and malnutrition.

The Great Seto Bridge in Setonaikai National Park
(YOSHIO NOHARA/WC)

For the Japanese population the end of the war brought the instant relief that the bombing had come to an end. However, immediately after the cessation of hostilities, the population struggled with severe food shortages and destitution.

Following the unconditional surrender on 15 August 1945, the Japanese state underwent profound changes. Japan's constitution was rewritten with a strong focus on pacifism as its military regime was dismantled by the Allied forces: importantly, the country was prohibited from rearming beyond a pure civil defence force. Controversially, **Emperor Hirohito**'s position was preserved: stripped of political power he continued to reign as the symbol of Japan's constitutional monarchy. This **Showa** era lasted until

Showa emperor Hirohito in ceremonial court dress at his enthronement in 1928
(EVERETT COLLECTION/SS)

The future Reiwa emperor Naruhito and empress Masako at their wedding in 1993 (MINISTRY OF FOREIGN AFFAIRS OF JAPAN/WC)

Hirohito's death in 1989: he was the 124th emperor of Japan and had reigned for an impressive 62 years. At the time of his death, he was one of the longest-serving monarchs in the world.

Showa was succeeded by the **Heisei** era under Hirohito's son, **Akihito**, a period which lasted for 30 years until he abdicated the **Chrysanthemum Throne** on 30 April 2019 in favour of his son, **Naruhito**. Under Naruhito, Heisei gave way to the **Reiwa** era, symbolised by the ideal of 'Beautiful Harmony'.

Throughout these post-war eras the Japanese have clung to their traditional customs: the government may have accepted unconditional defeat, but the ordinary people did not surrender their cultural identity.

Onomichi: A timeless port town and a portal to adventure

Along the Setonaikai shoreline, some 60km to the east of Kure and still within Hiroshima Prefecture, is the port town of Onomichi. Although wartime bombing devastated the nearby naval hub of Kure, Onomichi was spared due to its smaller size and rural surroundings.

Originally developed as one of Setonaikai's prime port locations in the twelfth century, the town was constructed over many centuries and its houses, temples and old alleyways have mostly been preserved. With its narrow strip of land between mountain and sea in the old quarters, the town's buildings cascade along the steep hills to create a quaint and anachronistic ambience.

OPPOSITE A dramatic red sunset above the bay of Onomichi (ROBERTHARDING/A)

A view over Onomichi from Senkoji (SOOJA GEN)

The resulting townscape is intimate and reminiscent of its history, attracting and inspiring travellers, writers and film-makers.

The famous Japanese film *Tokyo Story*, directed by Ozu Yasujiro in 1953, contrasts Onomichi's quiet, small-town charm with the bustling metropolis of Tokyo. The film successfully portrays the lives of ordinary people as they adapt to Japan's post-war transformation during the Showa period. Navigating to a new world order and processing inner emotional trauma came neither quickly nor easily, and the fact that the nation survived the upheaval and prospered is a testimony to its long history and survival skills honed down the centuries. The resilience of Ozu's characters in Onomichi is a dramatic portrayal of that national spirit of endurance.

Symbolising Onomichi's spiritual landscape is the Buddhist **Senkoji** Temple ('Temple of One Thousand Lights'). Standing high on a hill 150m above sea level, Senkoji offers visitors panoramic views of the town below. This sacred point shines out a beacon of hope and conjures up the sense of historical flow, capturing the continuity of life: a place where past and present meet.

Modern-day Onomichi is an important entry point for the scenic **Shimanami Kaido**. One of the world's top ten cycling routes, this is a destination which annually attracts large numbers of cyclists and other visitors from around the world. A series of bridges connect Honshu to Shikoku and offer stunning routes. Unassuming, provincial Onomichi has evolved into a starting point for an adventure. What a transformation!

Shimanami Kaido: Japan's scenic island-hopping trail

Photogenic and spectacular, the Shimanami Kaido connects Onomichi in Honshu and Imabari in Shikoku, hopping over six small islands linked by six magnificent bridges. Walkers, cyclists and motorists enjoy criss-crossing roughly 80km of well-prepared scenic roads.

While some cyclists speed along the route, others enjoy a more leisurely pace, stopping off at inns, temples and shrines, beaches and parks, galleries and museums and a whole range of eating places. The stunning trail features many essential waypoints, including:

- **Ikuchijima**: renowned for its lemon production.
- **Omishima**: known as the 'Cyclists' Holy Place', is home to a mystic Shinto shrine with auspicious trees, some of which are three thousand years old.

The Shimanami Kaido cycle route as it passes under the Tatara Bridge
(FLORIAN AUGUSTIN/S)

- **Hakatajima**: famed for its high-quality sea salt – the island's speciality salt ice cream is a popular refreshing treat, even in winter.

Not only is sunstroke a real danger, but the hot and humid summer months make cycling the whole route exhausting. At this time of year, then, a relaxed pace is advised, and ferry services from Onomichi or Imabari, stopping at some islands in between, provide a welcome alternative to cycling. The many bicycle-rental shops along the route offer additional flexibility. But, a word of warning: public transport on these small islands is very limited, so careful planning is a must!

Imabari:
The Sea Castle and industry

The Shimanami Kaido journey often ends on the northwestern side of Shikoku Island at Imabari, a city with unique stories to tell. Imabari offered strategic control of the Setonaikai, and its castle, built during the Edo period, exploited the location to great effect. Unlike typical highland castles, Imabari's, known as the **Sea Castle**, was built at sea level and has a saltwater moat fed directly from the harbour. The level therefore rises and falls with the tide, and locals are accustomed to seeing a variety of saltwater fish swimming in the moat. But when a shark was spotted, even they were surprised!

Imabari is not typically a pretty tourist town. It provides a convenient transit location for cyclists and travellers, and is also a regional industrial centre supporting local workers. **Imabari towels** in particular are renowned throughout Japan, popular as luxury presents during the summer

Ochugen and winter **Oseibo** gift seasons. The whole towel-making process can be seen at the Imabari Towel Museum, which is a little out of town but provides good facilities with an excellent restaurant.

Shipbuilding remains an important industry in Imabari. Although the city was almost totally destroyed by the wartime air raids, rapid post-war reconstruction soon led to the re-establishment of the city's bread-and-butter industries by one of Japan's largest shipbuilders.

Imabari has come to symbolise both resilience and fortitude, and offers a convenient stopover point for travellers and **Ohenro** pilgrims.

LEFT Imabari Castle (MUSASHI2001/S)

Ohenro pilgrimage: A route for devotion and reflection

The **Ohenro pilgrimage** through Shikoku Island dates back to the life and teachings of the Buddhist monk **Kukai** (774–835). This devotional journey has been compared to the world-famous Way of St James of Compostela, which concludes at the St James Cathedral in Santiago de Compostela in Galicia, Spain. The Ohenro journey may not take pilgrims to such a grand final destination, but it is highly flexible: while some pilgrims follow the numbered 88 temples in strict sequence, it is possible to visit them in any order. As a result, the 88th temple is neither the end of the road nor the most auspicious one. Such a flexible approach perfectly fits in with Kukai's unorthodox character.

Kukai was born to a wealthy and religious family in Sanuki, in the northeast of Shikoku (now Kagawa Prefecture). As a youth, he undertook strict **Shugendo**

The statue of Kobo Daishi looks down on a pilgrim at the gate house of the 42nd temple at Butsumokuji (JOHN STEELE/A)

training near Cape Muroto, where he claimed to have swallowed the morning star! At the height of such an intense experience, all that spread out before Kukai's eyes was the sky and the sea. Thus **Kukai**, meaning 'Sky and Sea', became his name. His reputation also lives on today through the culinary claim of introducing the popular noodle dish, **Sanuki Udon**.

Although Sanuki is far from the cultural hubs of Kyoto and Nara, Kukai's family was highly educated and well connected to influential people. Kukai himself was reputedly astonishingly intelligent (high MENSA class) and his talent was said to have extended to the ability to write with five fude brushes at the same time, using four limbs and his mouth! Although this is an obvious exaggeration, it is certain that Kukai was a calligraphy genius. Combined with his family connections, his exceptional capabilities qualified him to travel to Tang-dynasty China on board an official *kentoshi* envoy ship, in the year 804.

While such an envoy usually remained in China for 20 years, Kukai stayed for only two. During this short time, impressively, Kukai mastered the tantric teachings of Chinese Esoteric Buddhism, a Vajrayana tradition imported from India, from the Buddhist monk **Huiguo** (746–805). Following Huiguo's death, Kukai returned to Japan in

LEFT The 88th temple at Okuboji (SHIKOKU 4K/A)

October 806. His early return from China sparked suspicion and he was not allowed to enter the court in Kyoto for a few years. During this period, he remained highly active preparing to launch a new sect of Buddhism called **Shingon**, the 'True Word'.

With Kukai's spirited personality and tremendous charisma, Shingon Buddhism gathered pace around Kyoto, secured direct correspondence with Emperor Saga (786–842) and his court officials, and in time received permission to open the mountain retreat at **Koyasan**, in what is today Wakayama. Kukai's enduring legacy as a brilliant poet, calligrapher, painter, sculptor and educator established him as a cultural icon. Nevertheless, even today there is a popular saying in Japan: 'Kobo mo fudeno ayamari', meaning 'Even Kobo made mistakes with his brush'. The fallibility of humans and the importance of learning from our mistakes remains an eternal lesson, making us ever humble.

Kukai passed away while in Koyasan, in the final state of meditation, surrounded by his disciples. His revered status was honoured shortly after his death with the title **Kobo Daishi**. His teachings still live on through many Shingon temples across Japan, and believers recently celebrated the 1,250th anniversary of the Kobo's birth. Shingon Buddhism is the third-largest sect in Japan after the Pure Land and Nichiren sects.

Uchiko: A step back in time

Nestled in Shikoku Island's Ehime Prefecture is Uchiko. This quaint town offers a journey through the past where traditional crafts are preserved.

In its prime, Uchiko was famed for Japanese paper making as well as for candle production. In a traditional Japanese house, the doors and windows are made of **Shoji** paper, fixed in a wooden frame. In time, Uchiko specialised in high-end calligraphy-grade paper, and when fude-brush writing was standard, hundreds of skilled paper makers were kept busy. Alongside the paper makers, another group of artisans were employed making **Mokuro** candles, using locally sourced ingredients. With the advent of electric lighting and glazed windows, these traditional crafts inevitably declined. Candle making continues on a smaller scale, following the original formula, and provides a living memory of the town's cultural legacy.

From the late Edo period into the Meiji and Taisho eras, Uchiko occupied a strategic crossroads of trades across the region. Many merchants displayed their wealth through the construction of grand homes, and Uchiko residents enjoyed **Kabuki** plays and **Bunraku** puppet shows at the Uchikoza Theatre. This cultured lifestyle continued until the early twentieth century when war and modernisation transformed Japan, leaving Uchiko as a reminder of a much older age.

Although the traditional industry is a shadow of its former glory, visitors are fortunate to enjoy a picturesque destination with idyllic landscapes – green paddy fields, rivers, waterfalls, woodland and hills surround Uchiko. Blessed with such beautiful nature, the locals have worked hard to preserve the town's historical charms. The main street is a virtual living museum with cafés, restaurants and shops, providing travellers with a haven where they can slip back in time to taste a little of Japan's traditional past.

TOP LEFT Uchiko town (SOOJA GEN)

BOTTOM LEFT A living room from the Taisho era, Uchiko (SOOJA GEN)

Usuki: A history of maritime encounters

Located a 70km ferry crossing from Yawatahama (in Shikoku) to Oita Prefecture in Kyushu, Usuki is another Edo castle town, celebrated for its stone Buddhas carved into the rocks. This relatively minor fiefdom played an important role in early encounters with Europeans.

Located at the mouth of the Usuki River, the castle received a major refurbishment under Usuki's lord, Ohta Kazuyoshi, who was given control of the fiefdom by Toyotomi Hideyoshi (1537–98), the de facto ruler before the Tokugawa shogunate. Although the castle itself is now a ruin, the surrounding atmosphere is reminiscent of bygone days. In the sixteenth century, when the Jesuit priests from

TOP RIGHT The Usuki River, near the Usuki History Museum (SOOJA GEN)

BOTTOM RIGHT Usuki town (SOOJA GEN)

Portugal were active, the area hosted a strong Christian community, and Otomo Sorin (1530–87), the warlord of Bungo province where Usuki was situated, converted to Catholicism with the baptised name Francisco. With the protection of Sorin and other converted lords, Roman Catholic teaching spread quickly in Japan, and in Kyushu alone there were thought to be more than a hundred thousand Christians. Their faith and activity were initially tolerated by the ruling class, but following Sorin's death and growing concern over the missionaries' intentions, this gave way to harsher control or outright prohibition such that, by the beginning of the seventeenth century,

A representation of the *Liefde* (SOOJA GEN)

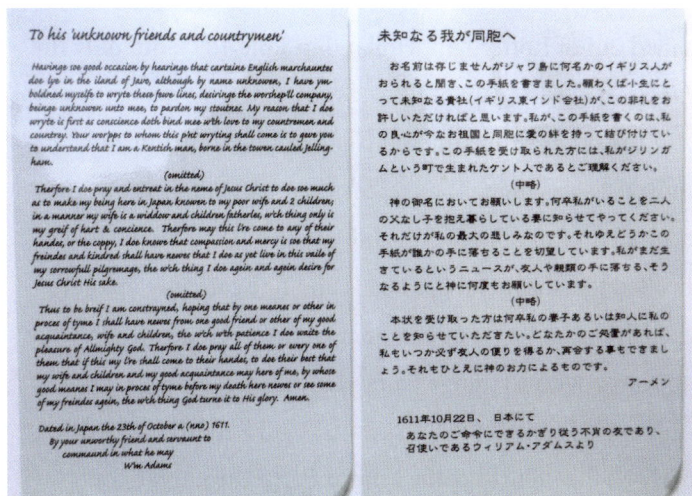

A reproduction and translation of Adams' letter from Japan (SOOJA GEN)

all Christian meeting places were shut. The persecution of Catholicism was clearly evident in Usuki, which was reduced from a thriving Christian centre to a place where not a single church remained. Sorin, at the height of his faith, sending his envoy to Rome from Kyushu, now seemed a distant dream.

The town would become internationally famous in 1600 when the Dutch ship *Liefde* ('Charity') anchored in Usuki Bay. The *Liefde* had endured a gruelling, four-month trans-Pacific voyage, arriving with a severely depleted crew which included an English navigator, **William Adams** (1564–1620). Adams' ship had been part of a five-ship expedition which sailed out of Rotterdam, Holland in June 1598, but only the *Liefde* made it to Japan.

The other ships suffered tremendous hardship and mortality was high. The *Liefde*'s crew was cut to 24, with only a handful of men still able to walk. They desperately needed the charity of the locals and one can only imagine their reaction to the appearance of their rescuers, men who appeared with a strange hairstyle (called *chonmage*) and dressing so unlike the Europeans. Usuki's Lord Kazuyoshi allowed the crew to come ashore and receive treatment. Despite this hospitality, six more crewmen died, reducing the survivors to 18. In the meantime, while anchored in Usuki Bay, the *Liefde* was inspected by the fiefdom's soldiers, who recorded the ship's inventory. For a merchant vessel, the *Liefde* was heavily armed with cannons and munitions, a necessary precaution given the conflicts between European nations battling for control of lucrative trade routes.

The story of the *Liefde*'s arrival was quickly transmitted to **Tokugawa Ieyasu** (1543–1616), who commanded the crew to be brought to him at Osaka Castle for direct questioning. As one of the few men still walking, Adams attended Ieyasu's court, together with a Dutch merchant travelling on the *Liefde*, Jan Joosten Lodensteijn.

RIGHT A portrait of Tokugawa Ieyasu by Kano Tannyu (1602–74) (WC)

Originally from Gillingham in Kent, England, Adams was now far from home and flung into the deep end of a totally foreign culture, as well as an incomprehensible language. But with the support of interpreters, Adams and Lodensteijn were able to answer Ieyasu's questions, particularly about European geopolitics and military methods.

The *Liefde* crew also had to contend with more familiar enemies in the form of Jesuit missionaries who accused the crew of piracy and even lobbied for their execution. However, having met with Adams and Lodensteijn, Ieyasu could see more value in keeping these ***gaijin*** (foreigners) alive.

During this period, Ieyasu had been planning for a showdown with his enemies, which culminated in the **Battle of Sekigahara** in October 1600. The arrival of the *Liefde* in Japan was therefore well timed: as a warlord and a brilliant strategist, Ieyasu would have appreciated the implications of all he heard. On the other hand, Adams' initial saviour, Ohta Kazuyoshi, crucially chose to side with the anti-Ieyasu coalition at Sekigahara, being more closely associated with the family of Toyotomi Hideyoshi, the former leader. Following the Tokugawa victory, Adams' and Kazuyoshi's fortunes were reversed. The tenancy of the Usuki Castle became impossible for Kazuyoshi, and by the end of 1600 he had fled Usuki and disappeared into the mist of history. This was a precarious and dangerous time for the *Liefde* crew and it was fortunate that Adams impressed Ieyasu to the extent that he became a trusted advisor, helping to shape foreign policy with the West. Adams and his remaining crew were also instrumental in passing on Western shipbuilding techniques by building two ships for Ieyasu. Adams was later honoured with the name **Miura Anjin**, the samurai title *hatamoto*, and a fief in Uraga (not far from present-day Tokyo), on the Miura Peninsula.

Ieyasu's victory started the **Tokugawa shogunate**, which lasted for some 260 years until 1868. It is also called the **Edo period** because the capital moved to Edo, where art and culture flourished among not only the privileged but also the ordinary people. From the point of view of peace and stability, this was an age comparable to the Pax Romana in Europe, and the Teragoya (literally, 'a temple's hut') schooling system made Japanese society highly literate when illiteracy was common in the neighbouring countries of Korea and China. Many children in Japan learned basic reading and writing, often free of charge, and the abacus was widely used to do simple calculations.

Adams remained in Japan for the rest of his life, despite repeated requests to return to his family in England. Instead, Ieyasu persuaded Anjin to start a new family in Japan and

Yuki, a daughter of samurai class and reported to be a Catholic, was introduced as his 'new' wife. She gave Adams two children, Joseph and Susanna, while his new-found prosperity also allowed him to support his 'first' family in England.

Compared with its samurai-dominated feudal past, modern Usuki is a tranquil, provincial town for visitors to explore. **Usuki History Museum** is an interesting stopping point, uncovering the layers of Japan's past from the Stone Age to the present day, and the area around the ruined Usuki Castle is now a popular public park, famous for its cherry blossoms in spring.

Beppu: Japan's hot spring paradise

Cradled between Beppu Bay and the volcanic peaks of Mount Tsurumi and Mount Yufu, some 45km north of Usuki, Beppu is one of Japan's most iconic **onsen** (hot spring) resorts.

The geology and volcanic nature of Japan is particularly evident in Beppu, which boasts well over a hundred spas. With a population exceeding 100,000, Beppu is one of the largest *onsen* resorts in the country and provides a haven for visitors to enjoy the thermal vents, which gush hot water and spew steam. *Onsen* bathing culture is one of the best-loved national pastimes, while visitors who prefer to marvel at the geothermal features without taking the plunge have the option of the **Hells of Beppu** tour, which consists of seven distinct geothermal spots, each offering its own unique scenery and atmosphere. Although these pools are dangerously hot for bathing, they offer a wondrous sight.

A hot spring in Beppu, one of the largest spa resorts in Japan (SOOJA GEN)

Bathing culture in Japan marks itself out from the custom elsewhere in the world. Visitors are kindly advised to observe the following, strict etiquette:

1. **No clothes** allowed: swimsuits are not permitted; bathing is nude.
2. **Wash first**: wash thoroughly and rinse before entering the shared pool.
3. **Keep quiet**: loud talking, running or swimming is strictly discouraged.
4. **Tattoo restrictions**: tattoos are traditionally prohibited due to their association with **Yakuza** gangsters, and are therefore off-putting to the public. The rules are becoming more relaxed as tattoos gradually become more fashionable, but visitors with tattoos are advised to check beforehand.

Beppu has much to offer in a single destination: the relaxing tranquillity of natural hot spring baths with an outstanding volcanic landscape and a beautiful view of Beppu Bay. The public transportation link is also excellent.

Kokura: A city of resilience and reflection

Kokura holds a uniquely endangered place in Japan's history, having twice been the intended target for the atom-bomb attacks in World War II.

The first brush with catastrophe was on 6 August 1945, as a backup target for the bomb dropped on Hiroshima by the Boeing B-29 Superfortress *Enola Gay*. Three days later, thick cloud cover and smoke (from the firebombing of nearby Yahata) saved Kokura from the second atom bomb, Fat Man. Another B-29 bomber, *Bockscar*, circled the city three times before abandoning the search for its target and diverting to Nagasaki. Despite these two escapes, Kokura remained an atom-bomb target until Japan surrendered on 15 August 1945. It was a close call.

Occupying a strategic junction, Kokura connects two of Japan's main islands: Honshu and Kyushu, in Fukuoka

Kokura Castle (SOOJA GEN)

Prefecture. In the twentieth century, when Japan aspired to become an imperialist power in the East, Kokura became a military stronghold, in line with its history. The world's first undersea rail tunnel, the **Kanmon Tunnel**, was completed in 1942 and stretches 3.6km, with over a kilometre actually under the sea. This triumph of civil engineering enhanced Kokura's role as the gateway into Kyushu and its importance as a hub for commerce, industry and military activity. Indeed, its munitions factory was Fat Man's intended target.

The beautiful Kokura Castle seen today has been reconstructed to its Edo-period grandeur. It was originally built by Hosokawa Tadaoki in 1602, who was rewarded with the Kokura domain for siding with the victorious Tokugawa at the Battle of Sekigahara. The most extraordinary warrior known to us today, however, is not Tadaoki, but a samurai called **Miyamoto Musashi**. He was 17 years old when he fought at Sekigahara in October 1600, where some 170,000 warriors were mustered in the battlefield and the cannons of the Dutch merchant vessel *Liefde* were also deployed. Musashi fought beside his friends in the 'West Camp' against Ieyasu's 'East Camp'. After losing his master at Sekigahara, Musashi became a *ronin*, an itinerant samurai: literally, a 'floating man'. In his wandering life, he won over 60 duels, with the most famous against Sasaki Kojiro in April 1612, known as the **Duel of Ganryujima**, near Kokura. To avoid a charge of murder, duelling required permission from the provincial lord, thus the tiny island of Ganryujima had been designated for the confrontation.

This tough encounter was Musashi's last duel, following which he dedicated himself to leading a more spiritual and cultured life until his death in 1645. Musashi spent seven years in Kokura, the longest in one place in his wandering life, refining his martial arts, calligraphy, artwork and writing. He wrote two books: *The Book of Five Rings* about

kenjutsu martial art, and *The Path of Aloneness*. There could not be a greater contrast between the traditional way of face-to-face battle, practised by Musashi, and the often indiscriminate, destructive force of modern warfare, with the atom bomb being its most extreme manifestation.

In 1963, Kokura merged with neighbouring cities, including Yahata and Moji, to form Kita-Kyushu City, blending a vibrant, modern metropolis with ancient tradition. A wedding ceremony, for example, is still popular

Traditional wedding attire (SOOJA GEN)

in **kimono** costume, but the reception afterwards would more likely be attended in Western dress. There are still many occasions in Japan when traditional attire is called for, particularly at a time of celebration. Kokura's **Gion Festival** is one such event: centred around the Yasaka Shrine next to the castle and celebrated each summer for the past four hundred years, it is enlivened with **Taiko** drums and various performances, as well as other cultural rituals.

The descendants of those who escaped the atomic horror have not forgotten Kokura's near misses. In April 2022, the **Kita-Kyushu City Museum of Peace** was opened, a symbol of gratitude and hope for a peaceful future.

Fukuoka City: Kyushu's vibrant capital

With a population of 1.6 million, the capital of Fukuoka Prefecture is the largest city in Kyushu and the sixth largest in Japan. Fukuoka City is the culmination of a merger between the smaller cities of Hakata and Fukuoka.

The port city of Hakata grew around the Hakata Bay, a result of its close proximity to Korea and China. From the port, an excellent ferry service can take visitors on a short trip to the islands of Tsushima, which are only 50km from the Korean city of Pusan. Hakata is also the largest transportation hub in Kyushu, from where the fastest **Shinkansen** trains, **Nozomi**, speed passengers to Osaka in two and a half hours and to Tokyo in five hours.

The mighty, Edo-period Fukuoka Castle is now reduced to foundation stones, some minor outbuildings and

OVERLEAF A view of Fukuoka City from the castle ruins (SOOJA GEN)

moats, but it nevertheless commands a wide vista from the high ground.

There is talk of rebuilding the castle to its former glory. It was originally constructed in 1606 by Kuroda Nagamasa (1568–1623) on a grand scale, because it was he who had led the key forces that brought victory to Ieyasu at the Battle of Sekigahara. His reward was the prosperous Chikuzen province, and Fukuoka was the new name he gave to the area chosen for his new castle. He became the first Fukuoka Hanshu, effectively as the founder of the Fukuoka Han (domain). Nagamasa was once converted to Catholicism together with his father, but under duress by Hideyoshi, the ruler of the Azuchi-Momoyama period, his Christian faith was discarded and in time he joined in with the Christian persecutions as required by the Edo shogunate, the subsequent ruling authority.

In 1871, when the Han system was abolished following the **Meiji Restoration** to modernise Japan, Fukuoka Castle was abandoned like many others from the Edo period. Its ruins within Maizuru Park now offer visitors a reminder of Japan's feudal past.

Fukuoka Prefecture as a whole has a population of over 5 million and occupies an area three times that of Greater London. In relation to Japan, it is middle ranking in size. However, zoom out and you can see that Fukuoka is situated almost equidistant from Tokyo and Shanghai, China, a thousand kilometres distant in each case. As a result, Fukuoka developed into a major conduit between China and Korea which placed it at the centre of key historical events. Within living memory, displaced people from the Asian mainland sought refuge in their hundreds of thousands. First, when Japan lost the territories of Manchuria and Korea in 1945, some 700,000 Japanese citizens suddenly needed to head home; many of those unable to make it back to Kyushu were caught and dispatched to Siberia by the Soviets. A second wave of refugees came during the 1950–53 **Korean War**, when the Soviet and China-backed army of North Korea's Kim Il Sung invaded the south, initially making it as far as Pusan, only a short distance from Japan.

Despite the eventual armistice agreement, technically the two Koreas are still in a state of war. The development by North Korea of nuclear weapons, and repeated demonstration of its ballistic missile capability, is a grave concern for Japan.

Modern-day Fukuoka City is a dynamic, cosmopolitan, prefectural capital. Special visas for international entrepreneurs and streamlined administrative processes have incentivised business start-ups and attracted foreign investment. At the same time, the city's cultural heritage is celebrated with enthusiasm through numerous annual festivals, of which the following are a few of the major ones:

The Kushida Shrine in Fukuoka (SOOJA GEN)

- **Hakata Dontaku** (May): one of the largest festivals in the whole of Japan, featuring 30,000 costumed participants and drawing over a million spectators, is a spectacle of music, dance and floats. On horseback, the 'Three Gods of Fortune' provide an auspicious start to the two-day event.
- **Hakata Gion Yamakasa** (July): recognised by the Japanese government and UNESCO as 'Important Intangible Folk Culture', this event is centred around the Kushida Shrine and features highly decorated floats

RIGHT A float at the Hakata Gion Yamakasa festival (PONTAFON/WC)

being raced through the streets. It is a very atmospheric and energetic festival in the height of summer.
- **Hojoya** (September): This week-long, thanksgiving festival held at the Hakozaki Shrine is steeped in over a thousand years of tradition and designated as an important cultural asset for Japan.

Fukuoka locals are well known for their love of noodles; ramen, champonmen and udon are inexpensive and popular. At festival time, hundreds of stalls line up around shrines and temples, offering tempting foods and festival souvenirs.

Another important cultural event is sumo wrestling. Every November, Fukuoka hosts the **Grand Sumo Tournament**, the famous **Kyushu Basho**. To provide an

A woodblock from the early twentieth century depicting sumo wrestling, by the print maker Gyokuha (FLORILEGIUS/A)

auspicious start, a special ceremony is held at the Sumiyoshi Shrine, reputedly the oldest Shinto shrine in Japan. Sumo is an ancient sport full of old rituals, one of which involves the wrestlers tossing copious quantities of salt inside the *dohyo* (the ring) as they confront their opponent: in this way a typical tournament is 'purified' by the scattering of some 700kg of salt.

Despite the tournament lasting 15 days, obtaining a ticket to the Basho is particularly difficult, especially for the final day, or Senshuraku, when the winner is decided. Each competitor needs to win at least eight matches out of 15 to join the winning group.

For the leading wrestlers, becoming a ***yokozuna*** champion (the highest rank in sumo) can be a passport to idol status. Some consider becoming Japanese prime minister a more attainable goal, without the dedicated training required to reach a high level of fitness!

Not all *yokozuna* are Japanese, however. The legendary Akebono, from Hawaii, was the first foreign-born champion, and the 69th *yokozuna*, Hakuho, hailed from Ulaanbaatar in Mongolia. Graceful retirement beckons at the end of a sumo's career, but it can be compromised by the extreme requirements of bulking up to become successful – Akebono died of heart failure at the early age of 54, in 2024.

Genkainada: Vital and historical sea of northern Kyushu

Travel back in time to the ice ages and you could walk across a natural land-bridge between Kyushu and the Korean Peninsula, such is the shallowness of the continental shelf in this area. Now, the shelf is covered by a sea, the **Genkainada**. This part of the Sea of Japan supports some of the richest fishing grounds in the world and is an angler's paradise. The Genkainada's long coastline, dotted with pine forests, sandy beaches and fishing villages, completes the scenic splendour. During peaceful times, the natural abundance in the Genkainada supported trade and cultural exchange between Japan and Korea. Unfortunately, just like the weather, this period proved to be a calm before the storm.

The Genkainada was the original route for *kenzuishi* envoys from Japan to Sui-dynasty China from the year

600. However, as political tension increased between Korea and Japan, *kentoshi* envoys bound for Tang-dynasty China switched to a more direct sea route which involved riskier voyages. Despite the loss of lives, Japan continued to send envoy ships to Chang'an, the eastern terminus of the Silk Road, for almost three hundred years until 894. The many sacrifices were balanced by the acquisition of Chinese treasures and knowledge that would eventually transform Japanese civilisation, including religion, philosophy, literature, astronomy and astrology, agriculture and technology, arts, politics and governance.

The lengthy and deep contact with the East Asian mainland put Japan at risk from forces operating there. This first became apparent in the thirteenth century during the **Kamakura period**, when Genkainada became the landing zone for the Mongol invasion armies of **Kublai Khan** (Genghis Khan's grandson). Kublai's purpose was to expand his empire (Yuan) beyond Mongolia. Koryo of Korea and Song-dynasty China had fallen and become vassal states. Kublai demanded Japan pay a tribute, under threat of invasion. The leadership in Kamakura initially tried diplomacy to indicate that they valued their independence. However, when they realised that Kublai Khan did not take 'No' for an answer, the Kamakura shogunate responded by executing Kublai's envoys.

In 1274, the first invasion forces landed around Hakata Bay but were fiercely resisted by a unified Kamakura *bushi* army. A larger Mongol invasion force of 140,000 soldiers and a mighty fleet of 4,400 ships launched a second attack in 1281; it was frustrated by enhanced coastal defences and the ships were famously scattered by a powerful typhoon, known around the world as the ***kamikaze*** (divine wind). Kublai Khan died before he could attempt a third invasion; the losses suffered by the Kamakura shogunate eventually led to its end in 1333. However, as a result of the successful resistance between 1274 and 1281, Japan was saved and has never been invaded.

Centuries later, Genkainada played a pivotal role in another massive confrontation with foreign forces: in 1905, the Straits of Tsushima were the site of a naval battle in the **Russo-Japanese War**. During this age of naked imperialism, Russia fought for control of Manchuria and Korea, but Japan was not prepared to be subjugated. The Russian military under Tsar Nicholas II had underestimated the modernised Japanese navy, a result of the government committing a staggering half of its national budget to the military. The Japanese destroyed the Russian Baltic Fleet in

LEFT The Genkainada laps a beach near Fukuoka (HACKENBERG-PHOTO-COLOGNE/A)

the Genkainada, marking a significant shift in the balance of power in East Asia towards Japan. Losses on both sides were heavy. Peace was mediated by US president Theodore Roosevelt (for which he was awarded a Nobel Prize), but the next 50 years would see the region plunged into two world wars and a big power confrontation in Korea. The Genkainada has witnessed many battles, but all their remains are now buried beneath the waves.

Hirado: Japan's portal to the West

To the west of Genkainada and accessed via the Iki Channel sits Hirado, one of 1,473 islands belonging to Nagasaki and the fourth largest in the prefecture. Its location benefits from cold water from the Sea of Japan meeting the warm water of the Tsushima Current and creating rich fishing grounds. (By the way, Nagasaki Prefecture has the most islands of any prefecture in Japan; Hokkaido comes a close second with just a few islands less than Nagasaki.)

Hirado offered a convenient hub for meeting European traders, a connection which built up in earnest in the sixteenth century with merchants from Iberia. They introduced not only Western merchandise, mainly in the form of guns, but a new religion, Christianity. The most prominent missionary in Asia at this time was **Francis Xavier** (1506–52), a founder of the Society of Jesus (Jesuits).

The port in Hirado (SOOJA GEN)

The restored Dutch East India Company building in Hirado (HKUSANO/WC)

Over a short period of two years, starting in 1549, Xavier established Christian communities in Hirado and Bungo Province (modern-day Oita), covering Usuki. Although a Buddhist himself, Tokugawa Ieyasu initially tolerated the foreign religion as the price for expanding trade with European powers. Later on, he became concerned about the colonial ambitions of the Iberians, allied to the spread of Christianity, and this anxiety came to a head in 1614 when Ieyasu banned Catholicism and expelled the Jesuits from Japan.

These were precarious times in Japan for Westerners. William Adams, as Miura Anjin, represented the Dutch interest in Japan, facilitating the opening in Hirado of the Dutch East India Company's mission. In the meantime, the English East India Company opened its trading post at Bantam in Indonesia, but the Dutch considered England a competitor and so withheld this information from Adams for fear of a conflict of interest. Eventually, Adams did assist with the formation of the English East India Company's trading post in Hirado. A letter from King James was carried by the company's Captain John Saris, which Adams translated for Ieyasu. The result was a free trade agreement between England and Japan, although coming a few years later than that with the Dutch.

William Adams continued to press Ieyasu to take leave to see his family in England, and whenever possible he sent letters to his wife, Mary. Before Ieyasu died at the age of 73, he did in fact grant Adams permission to leave Japan, but the latter's work on behalf of both the Dutch and the English East India companies delayed him and he was never to return to England.

Ieyasu was succeeded by his son, Hidetada, the second Tokugawa shogun. This change ushered in protectionism, intolerance towards Christian missionaries and a refusal to grant favours to the Western traders. With this change of power, Miura Anjin lost his privileged access and influence with the shogunate.

Adams died in Hirado in May 1620, aged 56, having lived in Japan for 20 years; fully 22 years had passed since he left Rotterdam hired as a navigator from Kent. His tombstone stands on a hill behind the Dutch East India Company building, and in memory of his life in Hirado, a beautiful rose garden has been created near to his burial place, looking out to sea. His will divided all his money and possessions into two equal parts, with one half bequeathed to his wife Mary and their children in England, and the other

Anjin's gravestone in Hirado (SOOJA GEN)

The Anjin memorial rose garden in Hirado (SOOJA GEN)

half to his children with Yuki, Joseph and Susanna. Joseph inherited his father's samurai title Hatamoto, together with the estate in Uraga on the Miura Peninsula, and also became known as Miura Anjin.

Sasebo: From fishing village to naval powerhouse

When steam replaced sail, the abundance of local coal combined with its convenient location (between Hirado and Nagasaki City) meant that the small fishing village of Sasebo was strategically placed to meet its destiny, becoming a critical naval base established in 1883. Not long after, it became the base from which Admiral Togo's Imperial Fleet set off to defeat the Russian Baltic Fleet in the Straits of Tsushima. The surprise victory lifted the national mood and confidence grew on the world stage but, ironically, the optimistic view of its power led the country to a more aggressive pursuit of imperialism: the Japanese Army and Navy rampaged for the next generation until the devastating defeat in 1945.

Sasebo's fortunes suffered a downturn later in the twentieth century with the demise of the coal industry.

The port in Sasebo (SOOJA GEN)

Although it narrowly escaped being a nuclear target during World War II, heavy conventional bombing destroyed half of the city. Following the Japanese surrender, the base was rebuilt for use by the United Nations and the USA and, when the Korean War broke out in 1950, Sasebo resumed its role as an important wartime naval base. To this day, the USA maintains its Pacific Seventh Fleet at Sasebo. This arrangement has been largely accepted by the local population, although protests were sparked in the 1970s due to the servicing there of nuclear submarines.

Although the post-war Japanese constitution prohibits offensive military capability, Japan retains the right of self-defence. A **Japan Maritime Self-Defence Force (JMSDF)** has been based in Sasebo since 1953, with a mandate to protect Japanese territorial waters. From time to time, Japan and the USA conduct joint naval exercises using their bases in Sasebo.

As we progress into a new century, once again regional tensions are rising. The commitment to peaceful resolution of disputes enshrined in the Japanese constitution is not shared by all its neighbours, and so Sasebo's military value still remains.

Balancing the area's role in times of conflict is some outstanding natural beauty, nestled as it is between lush, green mountains and the sea, with a part of the city falling within the spectacular Saikai National Park. Through the year the climate see-saws between a long, subtropical, humid summer and occasionally freezing winter. At any time of year, Sasebo offers visitors culinary delights, the most popular with Americans being the **Sasebo Burger**, a variation on the hamburger using local Sasebo ingredients. Of course, a bounty of fresh seafood, including sushi, is also available for diners seeking more traditional specialities.

Dejima:
Enter Japan's closed past

Unlike the other locations presented so far, Dejima claims a special status, being a manmade island measuring just 120m by 75m. It is really a tiny headland formed by digging a short canal. Compared with its small size, it commands a prominent place in Japan's history: during the long period of *sakoku* (isolation), Dejima was Japan's only trading post with the West. It was initially constructed in 1636 by the order of the Tokugawa shogunate to confine the Portuguese and to keep them under surveillance.

Previously, in Latin America, the Iberians had formed colonies using Catholic missionaries as an advanced guard. For some time, Tokugawa Ieyasu had permitted foreigners to settle in Hirado and to move freely in Japan. However, as Catholicism spread with the conversion of farmers, merchants and samurai families, Ieyasu's tolerance wore thin and he ordered the expulsion of the Jesuit fathers in

1614. After Ieyasu's death, the second shogun Hidetada and the third shogun Iemitsu ensured that any kind of foreign colonialism, particularly by Europeans, would not be permitted. In 1639, all Portuguese were expelled, leaving Dejima empty only three years after its construction.

The fate of the English East India Company was no less rosy. It lost the competition with the Dutch and closed its trading post at Hirado only ten years after it opened; its focus switched to China and southeast Asia. Not long after, in 1641, the Dutch East India Company was ordered to relocate from Hirado to Dejima. This area, about two football pitches

A nineteenth-century painting of Dejima, with the Dutch flag flying over the island (PICTURES FROM HISTORY/UNIVERSAL IMAGES/SS)

A painting of a group of Dutch traders dining at Dejima, c.1825
(PICTURES FROM HISTORY/UNIVERSAL IMAGES/SS)

in size and with a bridge connection to Nagasaki, was Japan's sole window open to Europe for the next two centuries, and the Dutch were the West's only representatives as a result of their exclusive trading rights. This limited portal did, however, provide Japan access to Western science, medicine and technology.

Inevitably, life in Dejima was claustrophobic: the settlement accommodated only a dozen or so Dutchmen at any one time, with some warehouses and living quarters for Japanese officials. Almost two hundred years later, in 1823, into this strange enclave landed a remarkable Bavarian physician, Philipp Franz Balthasar **von Siebold** (1796–1866), following his appointment by the Dutch East India Company. Beyond his medical expertise, von Siebold's curiosity and interests ranged far, taking in botany, biology, nature and art. He also introduced plants to Europe, including the hydrangea and *Primula sieboldii*.

Despite restrictions on the movement of foreigners, von Siebold managed to travel off the island, taking advantage of his status as a doctor and even treating some

Philipp Franz von Siebold, physician, botanist, scientist and collector
(PICTURES FROM HISTORY/ UNIVERSAL IMAGES/SS)

patients outside Dejima. He started a seminar series called '**Rangaku**' at Narutaki-juku in downtown Nagasaki, teaching Western medicine and science to eager Japanese students, a number of whom became prominent physicians and were instrumental in developing the practice of medicine in Japan. During his six-year stay in Dejima, von Siebold led an active life, busy collecting samples and a wide variety of artefacts. However, his curiosity got the better of him: forbidden items were found in his possession, critically a detailed map of Japan, and so he was expelled from the country, returning to Holland in 1830. He left a common-law wife, Taki, and a daughter, Kusumoto Ine (1827–1903), who later became the first female doctor in Japan to practise Western medicine. Von Siebold wrote three major books: *Flora Japonica*, *Fauna*

Taki (left) and Ine (right), Siebold's Japanese wife and daughter, depicted on a box with mother-of-pearl inlay (SIEBOLD MEMORIAL MUSEUM, NAGASAKI)

Japonica and *Nippon*. He was a true Japanophile and his substantial collections from Japan are a treasure trove, giving us a valuable insight into the time.

The long period of isolation eventually came to an end in 1854. American pressure to open up the Japanese market had been mounting for several years, culminating in the arrival of the US Navy's '**Black Ships**' under the command of Commodore Matthew Perry (1794–1858). At a stroke, the 260-year *sakoku* period of self-isolation drew to a close. At the point of Perry's naval guns, Japan agreed to open up the country to trade with the West, and Dejima's role as the sole trading post with the West came to an end.

Nagasaki: A city of faith, trade and resilience

Nagasaki boasts a rich, historical relationship with the West and its reputation should not be defined solely by a single destructive event in 1945.

When Tudor England was being tortured by political and religious strife, on the other side of the world, feudal Japan was also suffering its own persecutions based on the intertwining of religion and politics.

For the Jesuit and the Franciscan priests, backed by European monarchs with imperial aspirations, territorial expansion was the measure of success. Supported by the warlord Oda Nobunaga (1534–82), the 'Great Unifier', they enjoyed some initial success. However, the priests' diplomatic manoeuvring was stymied by Nobunaga's successor, Toyotomi Hideyoshi. He was particularly enraged by reports that the Iberians were trafficking Japanese and also

The 'Three Unifiers of Japan' (left to right): Oda Nobunaga, Toyotomi Hideyoshi and Tokugawa Ieyasu (PIEMAGS/A)

implicated in overthrowing the rulers of the Philippines, and as punishment, in February 1597, 26 Catholics, including 20 Japanese, were publicly executed in Nagasaki. They were later beatified by the Vatican and their deaths are commemorated today by the **Twenty-Six Martyrs Monument** and the construction of **Oura Cathedral**, officially the **Basilica of the Twenty-Six Holy Martyrs of Japan**.

After Hideyoshi's death in 1598, the Tokugawa shogunate's attitude towards foreigners and their religion was balanced by the benefits of conducting trade and acquiring Western technology: many of the priests were useful conduits, so some degree of tolerance continued.

However, Christianity was decisively terminated by a series of uprisings in the southeast of Nagasaki, in Amakusa and Shimabara. A combination of poor harvests and punitive taxes levied by the fiefdom's chief, Lord Matsukura, forced farmers (including *ronin* samurai who had turned to farming) to revolt in the **Shimabara Rebellion** (1637–38). Many of the rebels were Catholic converts; they chose a young Amakusa Shiro, a 16-year-old boy, to lead them. Some 37,000 people answered the call, but they faced a massive force of 120,000 warriors mustered by the shogun Iemitsu (1604–51). Despite the rebels' strong resistance, the rebellion was predictably – and brutally – crushed, leaving almost no survivors.

Lord Matsukura himself fared no better: he was beheaded and his fiefdom confiscated by the shogunate as a punishment for overtaxing his subjects and causing them to revolt.

The Shimabara Rebellion marked the start of *sakoku*, an extreme solution to dealing with the influence of Christianity. Only the Dutch were allowed access to Japan, for the following three reasons:

LEFT Oura Cathedral (9SOMBOON/S)

1. They supplied weapons to crush the peasant rebellion.
2. The Dutch restricted themselves to trade, not spreading Christianity.
3. They offered the shogunate a controlled window on the Western world.

With the exception made for the Dutch, remarkably, *sakoku* lasted for more than two hundred years, until America forced Japan to open its market in 1854, under force of arms.

During *sakoku* the Christian faith persisted in secret. At the end of this period, Edo was symbolically renamed Tokyo as the capital of a modernising Japan; finally, the Hidden Christians (Kakure Kirishitan) were able to resurface.

Churches appeared again, one of the most significant being the Urakami Cathedral. Tragically, Urakami was just metres away from the epicentre of the atom bomb. At precisely 11.02 a.m. on 9 August 1945, as a priest was taking confession, some 20 Christians who happened to be in and around church died instantly as the Cathedral suffered total destruction. It was rebuilt in 1959 as a symbol of resilience and faith.

RIGHT Urakami Cathedral, destroyed by the atom bomb in 1945 and restored in 1959 (SOOJA GEN)

The flagship Bunmeido *castella* shop in Nagasaki, which opened in 1900 (SOOJA GEN)

Nagasaki's melting-pot history can be clearly witnessed in its vibrant, modern-day streets.

- **The Chinese Quarter**: Where Chinese merchants and restaurant owners settled, their strong heritage is apparent, forming a little China Town.
- **The Dutch influence**: These privileged foreigners left their mark by introducing Western science, medicine, architecture and academia, known as **Rangaku** (Dutch studies). There's a no more Dutch-inspired street name than Oranda-zaka (Dutch Slope).
- **Portuguese treats**: These Iberians brought their Madeira-style cake, which was transformed into a distinctly Japanese, textured sponge cake called *castella*. The Nagasaki brand Bunmeido is beloved throughout Japan.

If you come to Nagasaki, an essential destination for visitors is the **Glover Garden**, once the residence of Thomas Blake Glover (1838–1911), an Anglo-Scottish merchant. He started out in tea and silk trading, but within a few years of arriving in Japan he had established his own company in 1861, aged 23. From this launch pad, Mr Glover played a key role in coal mining and shipbuilding, even finding time to start up a brewing business which later grew into the

A view of Nagasaki Port from the Glover Garden (SOOJA GEN)

Thomas Blake Glover, Anglo-Scottish merchant and entrepreneur (WC)

world-famous **Kirin Brewery**. His possibly greater historical influence, however, owes to his activity as an arms dealer, supplying the opponents of the Tokugawa shogunate, the old feudal order which was eventually toppled. The new Meiji government recognised Glover's aid in this venture, as well as his other entrepreneurial undertakings, with the coveted **Order of the Rising Sun**, awarded to people who have provided outstanding service to Japan. The Glover family's exotic and colourful life in Nagasaki inspired Puccini's opera *Madame Butterfly*.

From the feudalism of the Tokugawa shogunate to the constitutional monarchy, headed by the restored emperor,

A Kirin Beer advert from the Showa period (SOOJA GEN)

Japan navigated a turbulent transition; it was on the scale of a revolution in terms of the profound change to the way the Japanese regarded themselves on the world stage. Along the way, the proponents of the new order had to face old vested interests. Some heroes of change lost their lives. The reward for the architects of the modern nation came in 1889 when the Meiji government, echoing Western values, proclaimed a new constitution recognising civil rights and religious freedom.

In the twenty-first century, as found throughout Japan, along the streets of Nagasaki the traditional and modern sit comfortably side by side, offering an urban landscape blending churches, temples, shrines and other places of worship. Indeed, Japan's ancient history is replete with gods, reputedly 8 million **Yao-Yorozu-no-Kami** in the Land of the Rising Sun. Today, each of the main faiths has their place, even for the same individual throughout their life: a Shinto blessing at birth, a Christian wedding and, at the end of life, a Buddhist ceremony.

The ravages of one single, cataclysmic event in 1945 could not destroy Nagasaki's unique cultural heritage.

From Hiroshima to Nagasaki: A tale of bonds across an ocean

On a new sunlit day, dawn breaks in Hiroshima and wildlife and people stir, before the daily routine of commuting begins. On such a day, this normal, peaceful activity was halted in its tracks: at 8.15 a.m. on 6 August 1945 by the atom bomb known as Little Boy. Ironically, the bomb detonated above a medical clinic. Now only a plaque, so easy to pass by unnoticed, marks the location.

With just a fraction of its uranium undergoing nuclear fission, instantly over 70,000 civilians were obliterated. In the following months and years more lives were claimed by radiation sickness, with some estimates adding a further 30,000 by the end of 1945 alone. However, life finds a way to survive. On the ravaged earth, the vivid oleander was the first plant to bloom and was adopted as Hiroshima's official flower. A few camphor trees also survived, providing another emblem of recovery and the hope people needed to fuel their determination to rebuild their city. Additional aid was to come from a surprising source.

Early in the twentieth century, taking advantage of free movement under the new Meiji constitution, many Japanese, particularly from Hiroshima, emigrated to Hawaii, eventually making up half of the total population, the largest ethnic group. At the outbreak of World War II, the ethnic Japanese in the USA were considered a threat by their adopted country and this led to the internment of some 112,000 men. After the war, when news of the devastation suffered by Hiroshima and Nagasaki reached the 'Japanese Americans', they were unstinting in offering aid. This act of generosity helped forge a bond between former adversaries in the spirit of shared humanity. Japan's post-war recovery was shaped, in part, by this willingness to heal rather than dwell on the past and attribute blame.

On the political level, there is more to the relationship with the victorious USA than meets the eye, but that is for the politicians and critics to debate. One thing is clear: it helped Japan to become a Western-style democracy ruled by law, cherishing civil liberty and allowing its cultural heritage to bloom. As long as Japanese people exercise their accumulated wisdom, peaceful coexistence should take the place of a revenge mindset and self-destructive militarism.

Reflection: A rainy pilgrimage to Nagasaki Peace Park

Rain fell gently on the day I visited the Nagasaki Peace Park, a soft patter forming a calming rhythm on a silent background. Ascending the gentle hill, the neatly trimmed green hedges set a tone of solemn tranquillity. The central path was lined with commemorative plaques gifted by other countries, including a poignant statue from Russia of a mother and a child.

The rain continued as I approached the park's fountain, its surface rippling with the constant downpour. I was struck by an image of every raindrop as a tear for each victim of the atom bomb. The creation and use of such a weapon on human beings still defies comprehension and this reflection disturbed me profoundly. Despite the universal acceptance of their catastrophic potential, these weapons are relied on by many nations as a vital geopolitical tool. Most ordinary people oppose their proliferation, yet feel powerless to reverse it. The challenge of truly disarming the world, a task worthy of a Nobel Prize, remains one of the greatest responsibilities for future generations.

My journey to Nagasaki was a personal pilgrimage, providing the opportunity to understand the country of my birth from a new perspective. Your journey, even along the same path, will be different as you discover your own truths. This is the beauty of travel.

Throughout this book, a recurring theme has been the resilience of the Japanese people, an endurance forged by a long history of coexisting with a volatile natural environment. Earthquakes, typhoons and tsunamis have tested Japan's resolve time and again. Rather than yielding to despair, communities have learned to endure, to support one another, and to find harmony with the forces of nature. As samurai once turned to the quiet rituals of the tea ceremony to calm the mind, so too have generations of Japanese cultivated a deep appreciation of natural beauty and the four seasons, to gain equanimity.

That same spirit endured through the devastation of World War II. Entire cities were reduced to rubble, and yet the national focus shifted not to vengeance, but to rebuilding. Today, Japan stands not only as a member of the G7 advanced economies, but as a respected global partner and trusted ally for the USA and also for the UK. This achievement is a testament to the nation's capacity for recovery, ingenuity and collaborating spirit.

Whatever lies ahead, future travellers to Japan will witness Japan's unique culture, nurtured and preserved by its people over the centuries, and reflecting a deep-seated passion for its nature and the distinct seasons. It is a culture anchored in respect for harmony, diligence and civility. This island nation has proven its confidence to adapt and even prosper as the surrounding world changes, but always defending its historic identity.

The Peace Statue

Beneath the statue in the photograph of the Peace Park (overleaf) is a plaque installed by Nagasaki City, bearing the following words.

> This statue was erected by the citizens of Nagasaki in August 1955, on the tenth anniversary of the devastation of this city by the atom bomb. Thanks to contributions from Japan and abroad, the 10m bronze statue, which was designed by Seibo Kitamura, was dedicated as an appeal for lasting world peace and as a prayer that such a tragedy would never be repeated.
>
> The elevated right hand points to the threat of nuclear weapons, while the outstretched left hand symbolises tranquillity and world peace. Divine omnipotence and love are embodied in the sturdy physique and gentle countenance of the statue, and a

THE PEACE STATUE

prayer for the repose of the souls of all war victims is expressed in the closed eyes. Furthermore, the folded right leg symbolises quiet meditation, while the left leg is poised for action in assisting humanity.

LEFT The Peace Statue in the Peace Park in Nagasaki City (RICHIE CHAN/S)

Epilogue: Kindness in the floating world

The people of Japan are, by and large, exceptionally kind. Of course, as anywhere, there are exceptions, but a general sense of social consideration and good conduct seems deeply embedded in the cultural fabric. Yet even in Japan, the traditional spirit of communal kindness appears to be shifting, gradually replaced by the more individualistic ethos often found in Western societies. The modern mantra of 'mind your own business' may suit certain political systems or serve as a strategy for self-preservation, but left unchecked it risks descending into selfishness and indifference. As Mother Teresa once warned, indifference is the greatest enemy of humanity, a sobering thought for any society.

In my own travels across Japan, I encountered far more kindness than indifference. Whether in shops, stations or remote towns, people treated me with generosity and grace.

EPILOGUE: KINDNESS IN THE FLOATING WORLD

When I found myself lost in the complex layout of Nagoya Station en route to Hiroshima, a woman took the time to walk a considerable distance with me to ensure I found the correct platform. In Uchiko, Shikoku, the innkeeper personally came to the station to collect me and drove me back the following day, well beyond any obligation. When I arrived at the Usuki ferry terminal and couldn't summon a taxi, a kiosk attendant used her personal mobile phone to call one for me. Stories like these abound. Visitors to Japan often remark on such moments, and I hope this spirit of kindness continues to endure despite social and cultural change.

Three centuries ago, during the Edo period, a seasoned traveller named Matsuo Basho (1644–94) set off on an epic 2,400km journey, mostly on foot. Departing from Edo (modern-day Tokyo), he travelled north through Honshu and down along the Sea of Japan coast to Ogaki near Kyoto. A poet by calling, Basho came from a samurai family but chose literature over martial pursuits. He became the undisputed master of haiku and is still beloved today as one of Japan's greatest literary figures. His most celebrated work, *Oku no Hosomichi* ('The Narrow Road to the Deep North'), is a travel diary filled with poetry and meditative insight. During his arduous journey, Basho often relied on the kindness of strangers – villagers and fellow travellers who offered food, shelter or companionship. His gratitude for such gestures, recorded in his journal, continues to echo across the centuries.

Kindness is, in many ways, the truest measure of a civilised society. Wars, conflicts and social fragmentation can quickly erode this precious quality. It must be cherished and protected, particularly in what the Japanese refer to as Ukiyo (the floating world), a metaphor for life's transience.

At the end of this journey from Hiroshima to Nagasaki, it seems fitting to conclude with the words of Matsuo Basho, rendered into English by Donald Keene:

> The months and days are the travellers of eternity. The years that come and go are also voyagers. Those who float away their lives on ships or who grow old leading horses are forever journeying, and their homes are wherever their travels take them.

We are the eternal travellers through time. Kindness is most welcome wherever we are, and if freely given mutually, then Peace prevails. May the floating world we all inhabit be steadied by kindness.